NEW ORLEANS

NEW ORLEANS

Introduction by
Pete Fountain

Photography by
Arthur J. Klonsky
and

Jane Sobel

SKYLINE
PRESS

for Annie and Louis

We should also like to thank Patricia Chandler, David Messler
of the New Orleans Steamship Company, Rodney Smith and
the staff of the Soniat House, Dodi Spencer, Patricia
Whitty-Johnson, and all those whose co-operation made this
book possible.

Produced by Boulton Publishing Services, Inc., Toronto
Designed by Fortunato Aglialoro

ISBN 0-19-540622-2
1 2 3 4 – 7 6 5 4
Printed in Hong Kong by Scanner Art Services, Inc., Toronto

Introduction

NEW ORLEANS. I don't know if I could ever quite explain what's so great about this city. It's just a fine, fine place. I kind of doubt that there are many places that get in your blood like this one. It's like you can't leave it. You go somewhere else, and you have a little devil on your shoulder. Every time you think, 'Maybe this would be a nice place to try living,' that little devil makes you bite your tongue. And eventually, the thought never crosses your mind again. It's as simple as that—once you've lived here, there's no place else fit to live.

I guess everybody knows New Orleans as the birthplace of jazz. It's a big thing down here—in fact, a lot of people in New Orleans really live for it and nothing else. There are so many good music clubs that come Friday night when you want to take your girl out on the town, you can hardly decide which place to go. So what you end up doing is you go to a few different places. Spend an hour or two here, an hour or two there. Before you know it, the sun's coming up. People talk about how slow it is down here in the Deep South, and maybe that's true. All I know is the time sure does fly. One minute you're just having a good time, and the next thing you know it's morning and you have to go home and catch a few winks before you plan your Saturday night.

I know it's hard to believe, but people in New Orleans really do live that way. There's no such thing as too much fun. Take Mardi Gras, for instance. I know it's a crazy thing, but to me it makes so much sense! You build up to it for a couple of weeks, then Fat Tuesday rolls around.

Everybody takes the day off, dresses up as something or somebody else, and has the time of their life. The good vibrations in the air are something else; everybody's friends with everybody. Some people ride on floats in the parade, some people walk in krewes like my Half Fast Walking Club, and some people stand in the crowds and dance as it all passes by. Then on Wednesday, everybody gets up and goes back to work, and life returns to normal. But that one day just cleanses your system. After that, you can make it through the year until the next time. Mardi Gras is New Orleans dressed up (literally!) in its finest.

New Orleanians are always finding an excuse to be merry. We have St Patrick's Day parades and St Joseph's Day parades. We have neighborhood parades for the kids. We have festivals for shrimp season, oyster season, crayfish season, and a slew of seasons the rest of the world has probably never heard of. The Jazz and Heritage Festival is our biggest and surely our most famous, and it's two solid weeks of music and merriment. But all the festivals are that way—jam-packed with fun. If it's not a festival, we figure out some way to make a party out of it. We have parties because it's the heat of August, parties on Thursday to celebrate the next day being Friday, parties the week before a holiday to get prepared, and parties the week after because we can't bear the thought of it being over. We have parties on streetcars, and parties in the streets themselves. Where else do they even have jazz funeral parades? This is a city with *such* a tradition of happiness and good times with favorite people that I can't imagine anyone leaving for long. The ones who do usually come back despite themselves. Because of that, 'lifelong friends' are commonplace in this city that care forgot. This is a big city, but a small town in a lot of ways. It seems like everywhere you turn, you see some dear old friend that goes back to your childhood. There's a lot to be said for surrounding yourself with good friends.

Surrounding yourself with good food isn't such a bad idea, either. And in New Orleans we don't spare anything when it comes to eating well. The way we figure it is that you have to eat every day, so you may as well eat the best. Name what you want to eat and in New Orleans, we'll get it for you. Be it French or soul, Creole or Cajun, it'll be the best thing you ever ate. Ask for seafood, and you'll be whistling Dixie in between bites.

Then after you eat, go to the French Quarter. Walk around Jackson Square, take a look at the famous Mississippi River and the old steamboats that cruise it. Try out the coffee and beignets you've been hearing about. Peer into some of the fine old courtyards that are all over the French Quarter and you'll swear you're in the tropics. This city is green and lush all year 'round.

The French Quarter is only part of it, too. Visit the Garden District or Bayou St John and see the most outrageous old architecture you can find anywhere. Take a walk and check out the grass growing up between the bricks in the sidewalks. Grab your honey and fall in love all over again under the centuries-old oak trees that line St Charles Avenue. This is an *old* city. So many people have lived and died here. So many countries have settled here. You can see their melting pot of influences everywhere you turn.

Everywhere you turn there's something else that sets this city apart from any other, something else to love. New Orleans is a city of extremes and of excesses, but most of all, it's a city to love with all your heart.

PETE FOUNTAIN
New Orleans

1 Early morning in the French Quarter with St Louis Cathedral in the background.

2 Courtyard of Pat O'Brien's, well known for entertainment and a beautiful patio in what was originally a planter's home, the Maison de Flechier (1790).

3 *(right)* Bourbon Street at dusk.

4 Pete Fountain plays the clarinet most evenings in his club at the new Orleans Hilton.

5 *(right)* New Orleans Jazz and Heritage Festival.

6 *(left)* 1984 Louisiana World Exposition fireworks seen from atop the New Orleans Hilton.

7 French Quarter from the Royal Orleans Hotel.

8 *(left)* 'Swingers', New Orleans Jazz and Heritage Festival.

9 New Orleans Jazz and Heritage Festival.

10 Preservation Hall, St Peter Street, home to the purest classical jazz.

11 *(right)* The Soniat House (1829), Charles Street, formerly the home of Joseph Soniat Duffosat, now one of New Orleans' most beautiful small hotels.

12 Ray Tucker of the Soniat House
on Chartres Street.

13 (right) Breakfast off German porcelain,
Soniat House; whether it be coffee and
doughnuts in the market or eggs Hussarde at
Brennan's, breakfast in New Orleans is a
daily celebration of the city's charm.

14 Hermann-Grima House, St Louis Street, believed to have been built
in the 1820s by a wealthy merchant, with a fine patio and the only
still-functioning open-hearth kitchen in the French Quarter.

15 *(right)* C.J. Blanda House (1842), Esplanade Avenue.

16 *(left)* French Quarter façades.

17 Moon Walk, named after Mayor Maurice 'Moon' Landrieu, between Jackson Square and the riverbank.

18 *(left)* Yvonne LaFleur's 'You Boutique' on Hampson Street, Riverbend.

19 Library of 'Patty O'Brien's Creole Cottage' (1842), on Kelerec Street.

20 Toby Westfeldt House on Prytania Street, one of the massive classical mansions of the 'Garden District', so-called because of the extensive gardens surrounding the houses in this 'the American colony', by contrast with the European tradition of enclosed courtyards inside the Creole houses of the French Quarter.

21 *(right)* Courtyard on Governor Nicholls Street, French Quarter.

22 *(left)* Early morning, French Quarter.

23 French Market, Decatur and North Peter Streets; a tradition for nearly 200 years, first founded by the Spanish in 1791, remodelled in 1813 after a hurricane, extended again in 1822, 1872, and 1875, and with restoration still going on up to the present.

24 *(left)* Armstrong Park.

25 Neville Brothers at Tipitana's jazz club, down by the river on Napoleon Avenue.

26 Snooks Eglin playing at Snug Harbor, Frenchmen Street, adjacent to the French Quarter.

27 *(right)* Lloyd Lambert and the All Star Dixieland Jazz Band, Maison Bourbon, Bourbon Street.

28 *(left)* Carousel in City Park.

29 Flea Market, French Quarter.

30 *(left)* Sam Alcorn Trio performing at a Jazz Brunch, Arnaud's
Restaurant, founded 1921, on Bienville Street.

31 Beignets and café au lait (square French doughnuts and
chicory-flavoured coffee with milk), Cafe du Monde, French Market,
just across from Jackson Square on Decatur Street.

32 Garden District near the Audubon Park and Zoological Garden.

33 *(right)* French Quarter garden; note how the garden is enclosed in the Creole manner by contrast with plate 20.

34 Gateway, City Park.

35 Two-tiered fountain, in a style that ornaments some of the most beautiful courtyards of the South.

36 St Charles Avenue streetcar; one of the first streetcar lines in the world (1835) and the oldest still in continuous operation. The vehicles date back to the 1920s.

37 *(right)* St Louis Cemetery No. 2, North Claiborne Avenue and Bienville Street, a historic cemetery that contains the tomb of Dominique You, pirate-captain, and the grave of Marie Laveau, 'the voodoo queen'. Tomb burial was the practice in New Orleans because the ground was so water-logged. Tombs became so elaborate that Mark Twain once said the best public architecture of New Orleans was in the cemeteries.

38 Murray Herbert with crab, Kraemer.

39 *(right)* Bayou near Chack Bay.

40 Pelicans in the Zoological Gardens, Audubon Park.

41 Horse and buggy, French Quarter.

42 *(left)* Bayou Lafourche.

43 Fishing on Pearlington Bayou.

44 *(left)* Morning ride on the Levée near the Huey Long Bridge.

45 Oak Alley plantation house, on River Road, Vacherie; the
quarter-mile avenue of live oaks was planted by an unknown settler in
the 1690s. The present house is a Greek Revival mansion built in 1832.

46 French Quarter detail.

47 Chartres Street with St Louis Cathedral
(see plate 77).

48 *(left)* George Dureau, painter.

49 Piazza d'Italia, Poydras Street, locale of the Festa d'Italia.

50 Loyola University of the South, established 1911, conducted by the Society of Jesus.

51 Tulane University, begun as the Medical College of Louisiana (1834)
and the University of Louisiana (1847) and named after its benefactor
Paul Tulane in 1883.

52 *(left)* Orleans Parish Sheriff's Summer Camp at Samuel J. Peters High School.

53 San Francisco mansion, upriver at Reserve, a 'Steamboat Gothic' plantation house that lost its grounds to the encroaching river.

54 The *Natchez* paddle-wheeler, that cruises up and down the river from the Toulouse Street wharf.

55 *(right)* Pontchartrain (New Canal) lighthouse (1890) built on the site of a former station constructed in 1838.

56 *(left)* French Market.

57 Oyster Bar, Acme Oyster House, Iberville Street.

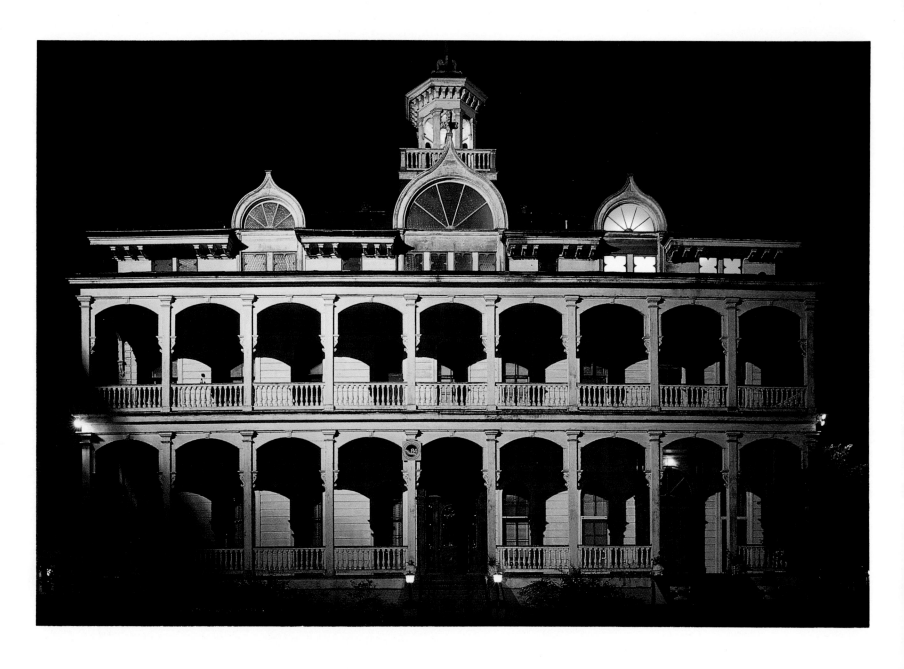

58 St Mary's Dominican College, St Charles Avenue.

59 *(right)* Camellia Grill, Carrollton Avenue near Riverbend.

60 Pontchartrain Bridge, six miles long, spanning the eastern end of
Lake Pontchartrain.

61 *(right)* Morning at the Fair Grounds, Gentilly Boulevard, home to the
New Orleans Handicap and the Louisiana Derby.

62 Galatoire's Restaurant, Bourbon Street, founded 1905.

63 'Fresh pecans', Evans Creole Candy on Decatur Street, a praline store
where the candies are still made in the same way as they were a century
and more ago.

64 Candy cart, 1984 Louisiana World Exposition.

65 *(right)* Ferris wheel, 1984 Louisiana World Exposition.

66 Lee Monument, Lee Circle; a bronze statue of General Robert E. Lee, Confederate hero, on a column of white Tennessee marble, dedicated 1884.

67 (right) French Quarter by night from the Royal Orleans Hotel.

68 *(left)* Downtown by night.

69 Crewing practice, early morning.

70 Sunrise on the Mississippi.

71 *(right)* Canal Street from the ITM Building.

72 *(left)* Louisiana Superdome, seating capacity over 56,000, seen from the top of the Hyatt Regency Hotel.

73 New Orleans Breakers game in the Superbowl.

74 *(left)* The river and the city at early morning, seen from No. 1 Shell Square.

75 Stern-wheeler on the Mississippi.

76 *(left)* The waterway at dawn.

77 St Louis Cathedral, facing Jackson Square (formerly known to the Spaniards at the Plaza d'Armas and to the French as the Place d'Armes). The present cathedral (1794) is the third church to occupy this site, and is named after Louis IX, patron saint of Bourbon France, as also of Louisiana, and of New Orleans.

78 *(left)* Jazz funeral.

79 Arnold Dejean, leader of Dejean's Olympia Brass Band, at a jazz funeral.

80 Mardi Gras, French Quarter.

81 Mardi Gras.

82 Mardi Gras.

83 *(right)* Bacchus Parade, Mardi Gras.

84 Merrymakers, Mardi Gras.

85 *(right)* Bacchus Parade, Mardi Gras.

86 Algiers, seen from the ITM Building.

87 *(right)* St Louis Cathedral, seen from Algiers.

88 Detail, St Peter Street.